THE THREE BEARS

RHYME BOOK

8/44

CL

THE THREE BEARS
RHYME BOOK

WRITTEN BY JANE YOLEN
ILLUSTRATED BY JANE DYER

Voyager Books
Harcourt Brace & Company
San Diego   New York   London

For Lui, who waltzes with bears
—J. Y.

To my mother, who first taught me to draw
—J. D.

Requests for permission to make copies of any part of the work should be mailed to:
Permissions Department, Harcourt Brace & Company, 6277 Sea Harbor Drive,
Orlando, Florida 32887-6777.

First Voyager Books edition 1997
Voyager Books is a registered trademark of Harcourt Brace & Company.

Library of Congress Cataloging-in-Publication Data
Yolen, Jane.
The three bears rhyme book.
"Voyager Books."
Summary: Fifteen poems portray three familiar bears and their friend Goldie engaged in
such activities as taking a walk, eating porridge, and having a birthday party.
1. Bears—Juvenile poetry. 2. Children's poetry, American. [1. Bears—Poetry.
2. American poetry.] I. Dyer, Jane, ill. II. Three bears. III. Title.
PS3575.043T47 1987   811'.54   86-19514
ISBN 0-15-286386-9
ISBN 0-15-201564-7 pb

A C E F D B

Printed in Singapore

The illustrations in this book were done in colored pencils and Dr. Martin's
watercolors on 140 lb. Fabriano hot-press watercolor paper.
The text type was set in Adroit Light by Central Graphics, San Diego, California.
The display type was set in Adroit Light by Thompson Type, San Diego, California.
Color separations by Heinz Weber, Inc., Los Angeles, California
Printed and bound by Tien Wah Press, Singapore
This book was printed on Leykam recycled paper, which contains more than 20 percent
postconsumer waste and has a total recycled content of at least 50 percent.
Production supervision by Stanley Redfern and Jane Van Gelder
Designed by Dalia Hartman

CONTENTS

 PORRIDGE

There are always three bowls,
And always three spoons,
And Momma Bear humming
Her wake-me-up tunes.

There are always three napkins,
Always three chairs,
And the great big yawns
Of breakfasting bears.

As far or as old
As I grow to be,
That's what porridge
Will mean to me.

THREE BEARS WALKING

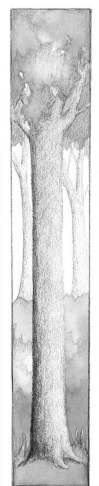

Three bears walking
down the lane, down the lane.
Three bears talking,
"Do you think it's going to rain?"
Three bears walking
to the wood, to the wood.
Three bears talking,
"Pretty day!" "Pretty good!"
Three bears walking
under trees, under trees.
Three bears talking,
"Do you know where there are bees?"
Three bears walking
by a stream, by a stream.
Three bears talking,
"Pass the berries." "Pass the cream."
Three bears walking
to their den, to their den.
Three bears talking,
"Great to be back home again."

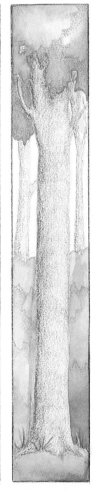

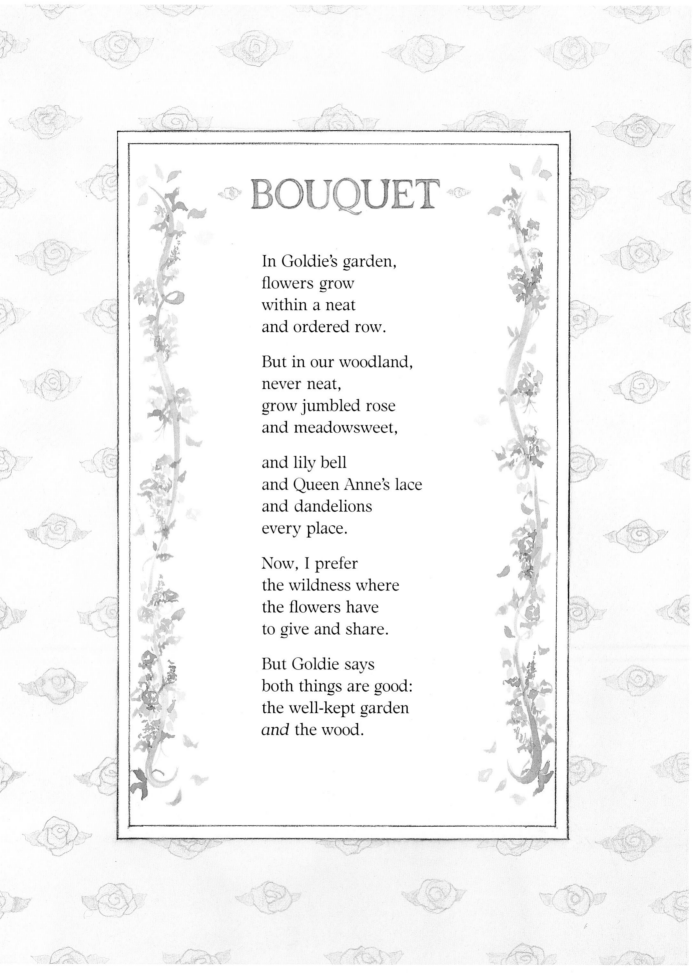

BOUQUET

In Goldie's garden,
flowers grow
within a neat
and ordered row.

But in our woodland,
never neat,
grow jumbled rose
and meadowsweet,

and lily bell
and Queen Anne's lace
and dandelions
every place.

Now, I prefer
the wildness where
the flowers have
to give and share.

But Goldie says
both things are good:
the well-kept garden
and the wood.

RAIN

rat-a-tat, rat-a-tat

There's a bear with a bunch of bright balloons,
And a pair of bears playing big bassoons,
And they're shouting out their favorite tunes,
Singing *Hip Hip Hooray for Bears!*

Now you may prefer being out on the sea,
Or in front of a roaring fire with your tea,
But the bears' parade is the place for me,
Singing *Hip Hip Hooray for Bears!*

CHAIRS

Some bears sit
in tiny chairs,
tiny chairs
for tiny bears.
Tiny chairs
can be quite tall
with straps so
baby bear won't fall.

But of all bears' chairs,
the very best
is to lie against
your poppa's chest
and cuddle up
to take a nap
upon the chair
that's Poppa's lap.

HOW TO BATHE A BEAR

1. Be sure the water's warm.
2. The bubbles fill the tub.
3. The rubber duck is there.
4. Find bear cub.

5. And quickly mop the floor.
6. Say: "Don't forget to scrub."
7. Feel for plug—and pull.
8. Dry bear cub.

Read to me riddles
and read to me rhymes,
read to me stories
of magical times.

Read to me tales
about castles and kings,
read to me stories
of fabulous things.

Read to me pirates,
and read to me knights,
read to me dragons
and dragon-back flights.

Read to me spaceships
and cowboys and then
when you are finished—
please read them again!

IN THE NIGHT

Goldie says
there are monsters in the night,
and they hide in your closet
till you turn off the light.
Then they howl and growl
just to let you know they're there.
But I'm not afraid
                                because
I'm a big bear.

Goldie says
that underneath my bed
there are ghosts that are people
who are not quite dead,
and a skeleton sits
in my rocking chair.
But I'm not afraid
                                because
I'm a big bear.

30

Goldie says
there's a vampire bat
and a vampire bullfrog
and a vampire cat
just waiting to jump
and to give me quite a scare.
But I'm not afraid
                          because
I'm a big bear.

But just in case
that Goldie may be right,
would you be awfully mad
if I left on my light?
If I slept in your bed
would you really really care?
I know YOU'RE not afraid,
                          you're
a great BIG bear.

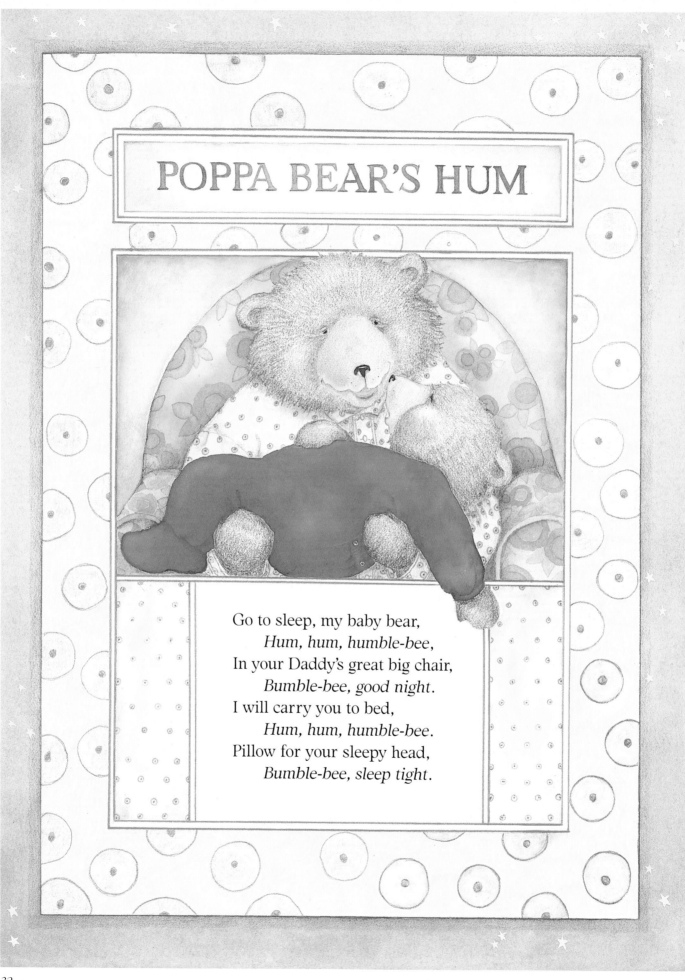

POPPA BEAR'S HUM

Go to sleep, my baby bear,
Hum, hum, humble-bee,
In your Daddy's great big chair,
Bumble-bee, good night.
I will carry you to bed,
Hum, hum, humble-bee.
Pillow for your sleepy head,
Bumble-bee, sleep tight.